Motivation

POSITIVE MINDSET ONLY

Decide To Commit To A Life of
Positive Thinking and Action
For A Happier You

Katie Lawrence

Table of Contents

Chapter 1:

The Power of Growing 1% Each Day

We all chase growth, we all chase success, but many of us want to be the best overnight, we want to get better 1000% over a month. We expect to lose 50 pounds by the end of the month, so we push ourselves so hard, so fast, so intensely, that we often burn out before the month has even ended. We apply this same speed to our relationships, our careers, other aspects of our health, and we soon wonder why we cannot sustain this momentum for long.

The reason is that changes must be made gradually. Sure we can go cold turkey by cutting carbs out completely from our diet, but how many of you will agree that by the 4th day, many of us will start bingeing on that big plate of pasta because we just miss it so much. If instead, we had cut our portions of pasta quota for the week by say 30%, how many of you would agree that it would have been a much better route to take instead of the former?

Today I want to challenge you to totally reframe how you approach change. After you have identified the areas in your life you know you need to work on, I want you to start working on one aspect at a time. Instead of aiming for a 100% growth and transformation by the end of next week, I want you to tell yourself that you will be a 1% better version of yourself each and every day.

This mindset immediately alleviates any pressure we have on ourselves for drastic changes. Changes that are unsustainable even in the short run. By making incremental changes, we give ourselves the space to grow, to learn, to get better, and to be better. Take your favourite sport for example. For me it's tennis. I don't expect to become like Federer overnight no matter how hard I believe I can. Instead, i break down each aspect of federer's game and work on fine adjustments to my own game 1% at a time. These 1% gains will compound over time. As with everything else that you do.

If career is an area of focus for you, instead of expecting to become employee of the month by the next month, work instead on becoming a 1% better employee each day. By the end of 100 days, you would've already become more than 100% than you were at the start of your job, and by the end of the year, you would already be so amazing at it that you would've believe how you got there in the first place.

Life is a marathon, not a sprint. If we sprint through life, we will miss all the amazing sights along the way. We will miss the fine details that make the journey worth taking. Similarly, our personal development and growth is also a marathon, not a sprint. We should all keep that in perspective when we approach any new project or endeavour. Only then can we truly make a lasting difference in the areas of our lives that matters to us most.

Chapter 2:

You're Good Enough

People come and say 'I did something stupid today. I am so bad at this. Why is it always me?' You will acknowledge even if no one else says it, we often say it to ourselves.

So what if we did something stupid or somewhat a little awkward. I am sure no one tries to do such things voluntarily. Things happen and sometimes we cause them because we have a tendency to go out of our way sometimes. Or sometimes our ways have a possibility of making things strange.

It doesn't make you look stupid or dumb or ugly or less competent. These are the things you make up of yourself. I am not saying people don't judge. They do. But their judgment should not make you think less of yourself.

No matter how much you slip up, you must not stop and you must not bow down to some critique. You only have to be a little determined and content with yourself that you have got it alright.

You need to realize your true potential because no matter what anyone says, you have what it takes to get to the top.

Need some proof? Ask yourself, have you had a full belly today? Have you had a good night's sleep last night? Have you had the will and energy to get up and appear for your job and duties? Have you had the guts to ask someone out to dinner because you had a crush on them?

If you have a good answer to any of these questions, and you have done it all on your own with your efforts. Congratulations my friend, you are ready to appraise yourself.

You have now come to terms with your abilities and you don't need anyone else's approval or appraisal. You don't depend on anyone either psychologically or emotionally.

So now when the times get tough you can remind yourself that you went through it before. And even if you failed back then, you have the right energy and right state of mind to get on top of it now. You are now well equipped to get ahead of things and be a better person than you were the last time.

You are enough for everything good or not so good happening in and around you.

Your health, your relations, your carrier, your future. Everything can be good and better when you have straightened out your relationship with yourself. When you have found ways to talk to yourself ad make yourself realize your true importance. When you learn to admire yourself.

Once you learn to be your best critic, you can achieve anything. Without ever second-guessing yourself and ever trying to care for what anyone else will think.

If you find yourself in a position where you had your heart broken but you still kept it open, you should have a smile on your face. Because now you might be on your path to becoming a superior human being.

Chapter 3:

Stay Focused

A razor sharp focus is required to bridge the gap

between our vision and our current circumstances.

Stay focused on the vision we want,

despite the current reality.

It's challenging to believe you will be rich when you are poor,

healthy if you are sick,

but it is necessary to achieve that vision.

Focus on the desired result.

Focus on the next step towards that goal.

Without focus on these elements there can be no success.

Stay focused on the positive elements,

solutions over problems.

The expected reward over the fear, loss and pain along the way.

What we focus on will become.

Therefore we have to maintain our eyes on the prize.

Be results driven.

Always focus on bringing that result closer.

Focus on what your grateful for.

Gratefulness brings more of that into your life.

Focus on problems on the other hand brings more problems.

If we focus on a big goal today,

we might not be ready yet,

but we will become ready on the way.

Commit to the necessary changes you know you need.

Get ourselves ready for that goal.

So many never act simply because they don't know how.

They don't feel ready.

We can achieve nearly anything if we focus on it.

Think carefully about what you focus on.

It is critical to both your success and failure.

Know exactly what you want.

See the odds of a successful happy life increase by unfathomable amounts.

How can we be happy and successful if we never define what that is?

It's not about what you are, or what you were in the past.

It is all about what you are becoming and want to become.

We cannot let circumstances or the world decide that.

We must use our free will and decide who and what we will become and focus fully on that.

Wishing, succumbing to the days whim, will never bring lasting success.

Success requires serious commitment and focus on that outcome.

Exude a fanatical level of focus.

Be exuberated in the pursuit of success.

The most successful often focus on work for over 100 hours per week.

They give up most social interaction and even sleep to make that dream happen.

They do not find this hard or stressful because they are pursuing something they enjoy.

Focus on something you enjoy.

Stop spending your time and energy on a job that you hate.

Work in an area you enjoy.

It makes focusing and achieving success easier.

Keep in mind that your time is limited.

Is what you're doing right now moving you towards your goal?

If not stop.

It is crucial that you enjoy your journey.

Start planning some leisure time into your days.

The goal is to remain balanced while you stick to your schedule.

If you focus on nothing, you will receive nothing.

If you do nothing, you will become nothing.

Your focus is everything.

Get specific with your focus to steer your ships in the direction of the solid fertile land you desire.

Aim higher as you focus on bigger and better things.

Why focus on plan b if you believe in plan a?

Why not give all your focus to that?

Stay focused on the best result regardless of the perceived situation.

The world is pliable.

It will mould and change around you based on your thoughts and what you focus on.

Your free will means you are free to focus on what you want and ignore what you don't.

Focus on a future of greatness.

A future where you are healthy, happy, and wealthy.

See the limits as imaginary and watch them break down before you.

Understand that you are powerful and what you think matters in your life.

Become who you want to be,

Not who others think you should be.

This shift is one of the quickest roads to happiness.

When you focus on what you love,

You draw more of it into our lives.

You will become happier.

You must focus on a future that makes you and your family happy.

You must stay steadfast with an unwavering faith and focus on that result.

Because with faith and focus anything is possible.

Chapter 4:

Becoming High Achievers

By becoming high achievers we become high off life, what better feeling is there than aiming for something you thought was unrealistic and then actually hitting that goal.

What better feeling is there than declaring we will do something against the perceived odds and then actually doing it.

To be a high achiever you must be a believer,

You must believe in yourself and believe that dream is possible for you.

It doesn't matter what anyone else thinks , as long as you believe,

To be a high achiever we must hunger to achieve.

To be an action taker.

Moving forward no matter what.

High achievers do not quit.

Keeping that vision in their minds eye until it becomes reality, no matter what.

Your biggest dream is protected by fear , loss and pain.

We must conquer all 3 of these impostors to walk through the door.

Not many do , most are still fighting fear and if they lose the battle, they quit.

Loss and pain are part of life.

Losses are hard on all of us.

Whether we lose possessions, whether we lose friends, whether we lose our jobs, or whether we lose family members.

Losing doesn't mean you have lost.

Losses are may be a tough pill to swallow, but they are essential because we cannot truly succeed until we fail.

We can't have the perfect relationship if we stay in a toxic one, and we can't have the life we desire until we make room by letting go of the old.

The 3 imposters that cause us so much terror are actually the first signs of our success.

So walk through fear in courage , look at loss as an eventual gain, and know that the pain is part of the game and without it you would be weak.

Becoming a high achiever requires a single minded focus on your goal, full commitment and an unnatural amount of persistence and work.

We must define what high achievement means to us individually, set the bar high and accept nothing less.

The achievement should not be money as money is not our currency but a tool.

The real currency is time and your result is the time you get to experience the world's places and products , so the result should always be that.

The holiday home , the fast car and the lifestyle of being healthy and wealthy, those are merely motivations to work towards. Like Carrots on a stick.

High achievement is individual to all of us, it means different things to each of us,

But if we are going to go for it we might as well go all out for the life we want, should we not?

I don't think we beat the odds of 1 in 400 trillion to be born, just to settle for mediocrity, did we?

Being a high achiever is in your DNA , if you can beat the odds , you can beat anything.

It is all about self-belief and confidence, we must have the confidence to take the action required and often the risk.

Risk is difficult for people and it's a difficult tight rope to walk. The line between risk and recklessness is razor thin.

Taking risks feels unnatural, not surprisingly as we all grew up in a health and safety bubble with all advice pointing towards safe and secure ways.

But the reward is often in the risk and sometimes a leap of blind faith is required. This is what stops most of us - the fear of the unknown.

The truth is the path to success is foggy and we can only ever see one step ahead , we have to imagine the result and know it's somewhere down this foggy path and keep moving forward with our new life in mind.

Know that we can make it but be aware that along the path we will be met by fear , loss and pain and the bigger our goal the bigger these monsters will be.

The top achievers financially are fanatical about their work and often work 100+ hours per week.

Some often work day and night until a project is successful.

Being a high achiever requires giving more than what is expected, standing out for the high standard of your work because being known as number 1 in your field will pay you abundantly.

Being an innovator, thinking outside the box for better practices, creating superior products to your competition because quality is more rewarding than quantity.

Maximizing the quality of your products and services to give assurance to your customers that your company is the number 1 choice.

What can we do differently to bring a better result to the table and a better experience for our customers?

We must think about questions like that because change is inevitable and without thinking like that we get left behind, but if we keep asking that, we can successfully ride the wave of change straight to the beach of our desired results.

The route to your success is by making people happy because none of us can do anything alone, we must earn the money and to earn it we must make either our employers or employees and customers happy.

To engage in self-promotion and positive interaction with those around us, we must be polite and positive with everyone, even with our competition.

Because really the only competition is ourselves and that is all we should focus on.

Self-mastery, how can I do better than yesterday?

What can I do different today that will improve my circumstances for tomorrow.

Little changes add up to a big one.

The belief and persistence towards your desired results should be 100%, I will carry on until... is the right attitude.

We must declare to ourselves that we will do this , we don't yet know how but we know that we will.

Because high achievers like yourselves know that to make it you must endure and persist untill you win.

High achievers have an unnatural grit and thick skin , often doing what others won't, putting in the extra hours when others don't.

After you endure loss and conquer pain , the sky is the limit, and high achievers never settle until they are finished.

Chapter 5:

Learning To Trust Others

Today we're going to talk about a topic that has the potential to make or break your working relationships or personal relationships with others.

Trust is something that consistently ranks on the top of relationship goals and it has very good reasons for that. Without trust there is basically no foundation. When you can't trust someone, it basically means that you don't believe they can be left alone without your supervision. If you don't trust someone to do the work you have passed along to them, basically it means you are either micro-managing them all day long or that you might just end up doing the work entirely yourself because you don't believe that they can do a job up to your expectations. How many of you have experienced bosses who are micro-managers like that? Basically it either means that they think they can do a better job or that they don't trust you to do the work at all. And we all hate bosses who are like that. Look into mirror like that now, are you doing that to someone at your workplace now?

If you don't trust someone in a relationship, basically you don't believe that they can't be left to their own devices either if they are out of your sight. You start to worry about what they might do when you're gone. If a partner has cheated on you before, I bet that trust has probably gone out the window and it might take a lot of time and energy to actually start trusting that person again. If you don't trust a friend, you might not want to tell them secrets for fear that they may go round sharing it with others without your consent. That plays into the concept of trustworthiness as well. It all comes in a package.

To build trust, we have to earn it. With our actions we can show others that we can be trusted with information, secrets, work, to be faithful, and to do right thing at all times. But trust works both ways as well. If we want people to trust us, we must be willing to extend the trust to others as well. If others have displayed level of competency, we need to start learning to trust that they can get the work done without breathing down their necks all times of the day. If however they come back with shoddy work, maybe you might want to keep a closer eye on them before you feel that their work is up to your standards.

Let others prove to you otherwise by giving them the benefit of the doubt first and then assessing their abilities after.

When you show others that you trust them to do a task, more often than not they will feel a sense of urgency and responsibility to get the work done properly and promptly so that they can show you that they are capable. To show you that they are competent and worthy of the trust that you have placed in them. When you can learn to trust can you truly let go and live life freely. Always having to micro-manage others can not only hurt your reputation as "that guy" but also allow you to have more time do focus on areas where your attention is really required. When you can learn to trust can you truly expand and grow a team, business, company, friendships, and relationships.

I challenge each and everyone of you to learn to trust others and not feel like you have to manage everyone around you to the granular level. If you feel that you have trust issues, for whatever reason, consider working on it or maybe even seeking help. Trust issues usually stems from a past traumatic event or experience that may have impacted your ability to trust again. If so you may one to dig deeper to discover the root of the problem and work through it till the feeling goes away.

Chapter 6:

Twenty Percent of Effort Produces 80% of Results

Today we're going to talk about the 80-20 rule and how you can apply it to your life for great results in whatever you are doing. For the purposes of this video we are going to use income as a measurement of success. This will directly translate to productivity and the areas that you are spending your most time and energy.

Have you ever wondered why no matter how much time you end up working, that your paycheck never seems to rise? That your income and finance seems to be stagnant? Or have you ever wondered, for those of you who have ventured into creating a second or third stream of income on the side, that you might actually spend lesser on those activities and earn a bigger income in proportion to the time you actually spent to run those side businesses?

This is where the 80-20 rule comes into play. For those that have not seen their bank account or income grow despite the immense amount of effort put it, It may be that 80% of time you are spending it doing things that actually have little or no change to the growth of your networth. The work simply isn't actually worth 80% of your attention.

Rather you may want to look elsewhere, to that 20%, if you want to see real change. I would recommend that instead of banging your head against the wall at your day job, try looking for something to do on the side. It may be just your passion, or it may be something you foresee greater potential returns. Start taking action on those things. It could be the very thing that you were searching for this whole time. If the rule applies, you should be spending majority of your time and energy into this 20%. By focusing on the tasks that has the greatest rewards, you are working smart instead of working hard now. Only when you can identify what exactly those tasks are can you double down on them for great success.

There were times in my life that I spent a lot of my time trying to force something to work. But no matter how hard I tried, I just couldn't see a breakthrough. It was only after further exploration through trials and errors did I finally come up with a set list of tasks that I knew were profitable. That if I kept doing them over and over again I would be able to grow my wealth consistently. By spending all of my time doing these specific tasks, I was able to eliminate all the noise and to focus my actions to a narrow few. And I was surprised at the outsized rewards it brought me.

If you know that something isn't working, don't be afraid to keep looking, trying, and exploring other ways. Keep a close tab on the time you spend in these areas and the income that flows in. Only when you measure everything can you really know where you are going wrong and where you are going right.

Remember that 20% of the effort produces 80% of the results. So I challenge all of you to stop spending 80% of the effort doing things that only produce 20% of the results. It is better to work smart than to work hard. Trust me. I believe that you will be able to find what those things are if you put your mind to it.

Chapter 7:

Why You Are Amazing

When was the last time you told yourself that you were amazing? Was it last week, last month, last year, or maybe not even once in your life?

As humans, we always seek to gain validation from our peers. We wait to see if something that we did recently warranted praise or commendation. Either from our colleagues, our bosses, our friends, or even our families. And when we don't receive those words that we expect them to, we think that we are unworthy, or that our work just wasn't good enough. That we are lousy and under serving of praise.

With social media and the power of the internet, these feelings have been amplified. For those of us that look at the likes on our Instagram posts or stories, or the number of followers on Tiktok, Facebook, or Snapchat, we allow ourselves to be subjected to the validation of external forces in order to qualify our self-worth. Whether these are strangers who don't know you at all, or whoever they might be, their approval seems to matter the most to us rather than the approval we can choose to give ourselves.

We believe that we always have to up our game in order to seek happiness. Everytime we don't get the likes, we let it affect our mood for the rest of the day or even the week.

Have you ever thought of how wonderful it is if you are your best cheerleader in life? If the only validation you needed to seek was from yourself? That you were proud of the work you put out there, even if the world disagrees, because you know that you have put your heart and soul into the project and that there was nothing else you could have done better in that moment when you were producing that thing?

I am here to tell you that you are amazing because only you have the power to choose to love yourself unconditionally. You have the power to tell yourself that you are amazing. and that you have the power to look into yourself and be proud of how far you came in life. To be amazed by the things that you have done up until this point, things that other people might not have seen, acknowledged, or given credit to you for. But you can give that credit to yourself. To pat yourself on the back and say "I did a great job".

I believe that we all have this ability to look inwards. That we don't need external forces to tell us we are amazing because deep down, we already know we are.

If nobody else in the world loves you, know that I do. I love your courage, your bravery, your resilience, your heart, your soul, your commitment, and your dedication to live out your best life on this earth. Tell yourself each and everyday that you deserve to be loved, and that you are loved.

Go through life fiercely knowing that you don't need to seek happiness, validations, and approval from others. That you have it inside you all along and that is all you need to keep going.

Chapter 8:

If You Commit to Nothing, You'll Be Distracted By Everything

I don't think anyone in their right mind would like to face a challenge where they have a chance to face failure or even a possibility of it.

We all need a new lesson to learn. A lesson of commitment and conviction. A lesson of integrity, grit, and sheer will. One might ask, why should I adopt the features of a soldier rather than a normal social being. Why do I need to go to extremes?

The answer to these questions is simple yet heavy, with a load most people avoid their whole life.

We all have somewhat similar goals. We all want to be in a better place in better shape. We all want wealth. We all want healthy stable relationships. We all want respect and a million other things.

Ask yourself this; Have you ever actually tried hard enough for any of this to happen. Have you ever tried to dig deep till you found your last breath? But it felt good because you had a good enough reason and passion to pursue?

The goals of life are a compulsion to have. We all must have something to strive for. Something worth fighting for. Something we can look back and be happy about.

But having a goal and committing to it are two different things.

One can have a goal and still not be motivated enough to do anything in their power to achieve that thing. No matter how the road takes turns.

We need to have the inspiration to drive us through the rough patches of life. To make us keep pushing even if we get squeezed within the incidents happening around us.

Don't take this the wrong way but you have to accept the fact that whatever you are feeling has nothing to do with what you want to achieve. Because what you want to achieve is something that your life depends on. The goals you set aren't some wishes or a feeling that your gut gives you. These goals are the requirements of life with which you can finally say lived a happy successful life. And this statement is the ultimate purpose of your life.

You were given this life because you had the energy to go for things that weren't easy, but you had the potential to achieve these. All you needed was a little commitment and Zero distractions.

The commitment you need isn't a feeling that goes and on and off like a switch. Rather a distinct key for the lock of your life.

So if you still think you will have days where you can try one more time, Let me be clear; You better start thinking about the future of your next generation. Because I don't think they'd have one.

You need to be committed enough to do anything that takes you closer and closer to your goals and nothing that wastes a second out of your life.

Because either you go all in or you walk the line and hedge your bets. The bet here being your life.

Chapter 9:

How To Set Smart Goals

Setting your goals can be a tough choice. It's all about putting your priorities in such a way that you know what comes first for you. It's imperative to be goal-oriented to set positive goals for your present and future. You should be aware of your criteria for setting your goals. Make sure your plan is attainable in a proper time frame to get a good set of goals to be achieved in your time. You would need hard work and a good mindset for setting goals. Few components can help a person reach their destination. Control what you choose because it will eternally impact your life.

To set a goal to your priority, you need to know what exactly you want. In other words, be specific. Be specific in what matters to you and your goal. Make sure that you know your fair share of details about your idea, and then start working on it once you have set your mind to it. Get a clear vision of what your goal is. Get a clear idea of your objective. It is essential to give a specification to your plan to set it according to your needs.

Make sure you measure your goals. As in, calculate the profit or loss. Measure the risks you are taking and the benefits you can gain from them. In simple words, you need to quantify your goals to know what order to set them into. It makes you visualize the amount of time it will take or the energy to reach the finish line. That way, you can calculate your goals and their details. You need to set your mind on the positive technical growth of your goal. That is an essential step to take to put yourself to the next goal as soon as possible.

If you get your hopes high from the start, it may be possible that you will meet with disappointment along the way. So, it would be best if you made sure that your goals are realistic and achievable. Make sure your goal is within reach. That is the reality check you need to force in your mind that is your goal even attainable? Just make sure it is, and everything will go as planned. It doesn't mean to set small goals. There is a difference between big goals and unrealistic goals. Make sure to limit your romantic goals, or else you will never be satisfied with your achievement.

Be very serious when setting your goals, especially if they are long-term goals. They can impact your life in one way or another. It depends on you how you take it. Make sure your goals are relevant. So, that you can gain real benefit from your goals. Have your fair share of profits from your hard work and make it count. Always remember why the goal matters to you. Once you get the fundamental idea of why you need this goal to be achieved, you can look onto a bigger picture in the frame. If it doesn't feel relevant, then there is no reason for you to continue working for. Leave it as it is if it doesn't give you what you applied for because it will only drain your energy and won't give you a satisfactory outcome.

Time is an essential thing to keep in focus when working toward your goals. You don't want to keep working on one thing for too long or too short. So, keep a deadline. Keep a limit on when to work on your goal. If it's worth it, give it your good timer, but if not, then don't even waste a second on it. They are just some factors to set your goals for a better future. These visionary goals will help you get through most of the achievements you want to get done with.

Chapter 10:

Friendship The Key To Happiness

Today we're going to talk about the power of friendship and why i believe everyone needs to have at least 1 or 2 close friends in their lives to make life actually meaningful and worth living.

You see, for many years while i was working hard towards my goals, i spent almost all of my time on my business and little to zero time on building Long lasting relationships. And this one sided approach to success left me with a hole that weakened me emotionally, but also physically as well.

In this very myopic view of what I felt success should be and what I felt i needed to do at that point, I prioritised my career first over everything else, neglecting my own personal health, family, and friends. Whenever I was invited for a meal or an outing I always declined, viewing that it was a waste of time. That it was taking time away from my work that i should be focusing on. And as I declined more and more of these offers from friends, the invite also became less and less frequent as they saw me as someone who was either too busy, or just didn't bother to want to take this friendship to the next level.

For a while I was actually happy, that i remember telling myself that yes I dont have plans for the week and that i can focus on my work wholeheartedly. But what i failed to realise was that I was prioritise making money over everything else. And that i was losing the connection with other humans. I started to become more withdrawn, more introverted, and I was losing that spark that i once had when conversing with friends. I wasn't experiencing life enough to have any meaningful moments that I could look back on and say that wow those were great times.

It all became one giant blur and 3 years later, it felt truly pointless. I found myself lonely and without someone I could talk to. I even neglected my best friend to the point that we drifted so far apart that she found other people to confide into. This left me with a sinking feeling that I had failed to prioritise The people around me.

And from that point on I knew i needed to change. I knew i needed to put myself out there once again and shift my priorities to the things that truly mattered. Friends that could ask you out for a quick meal so that you could hash out some of your grievances in life, friends that you can share your happiness as well as your sadness, friends that could provide some meaning to the days you were living, and even more simply, friends that you can count on when all else fails.

You see the business that I spent 3 years building collapsed on me. And I found myself with nothing to show for it. No experiences worth highlighting. Only regrets that I had failed to put others before my selfish needs.

It was a hard climb back to establishing the friendships I once had. People had already started viewing me as a flaker and a no-show that it was now up to me to prove to them that I was open and available to be called a reliable friend once again. Some efforts on my part did not go as I had planned but I kept trying to make new connections, joining new groups, making tennis friends, starting up conversations with new people and asking if they could invite me along to an outing. And these little seeds started to show fruition. I soon found myself getting asked out for meals and games, and life started to feel a little bit better again.

After the initial struggle, the floodgates starting opening and I found myself busy with true life again, connecting with other people on a deep personal and emotional level. And i felt that that was what life was really all about. Friends that you can see yourself hanging out 40 years down the road when you are old and nobody wants you anymore.

I plan to keep sowing these seeds for as long as life allows me and I challenge each and everyone of you to do the same. Businesses and careers may not last, but hopefully the friends that you have made will.

Chapter 11:
Feeling That You Don't Have Enough Time

Today we're going to talk about a topic that I think many of us struggle with, myself included. The topic is about feeling that we don't have enough time to do the things that we need to do.

Personally I feel this one a daily basis, and it is partly because of my expectations versus reality. Many a times I set unrealistic expectations of how much time is required to do a particular task on my list that I tend to pack my schedule with way too many items. This leads me to feeling incredible overwhelm and stress because it just doesn't seem like I can get all my objectives down before 12am. We tend to underestimate the amount of time and energy that working on our goals require of us that many times we end up setting ourselves up for failure.

I would watch the clock go by minute by minute, hour by hour, only to find myself still working on the very first task on my list of 10 things to do. As you can already imagine I end up feeling that I'm not being productive, even though most of the time I am, and this feeling that I'm not doing things fast enough erodes my motivation further.

There are times when I am genuinely unproductive - like when I get lost in watching television, browsing the web, playing with my dog, being distracted for the sake of procrastination, and a myriad of reasons. But for the purposes of this topic, I will not be addressing those issues. I want to turn our attention to what we can actually accomplish if given enough time, assuming our level of productivity isnt affected by distractions.

The first thing we have to realise is that the things that we need to get done will take however long it needs to get done. Many times we may not be able to control or accurately measure the duration that a task may take. Instead of setting a time limit on a task, we should instead measure our productivity and be focused on doing rather than completing.

As an entrepreneur, I've come to learn that my work never ends. When I think I have finished one task, another one just comes crashing onto my desk like a meteor - another fire I have to put out, another problem I have to solve. I've come to realise that once I set a deadline for the time I need to complete something, rarely will I ever get it done on time. Most often I will be off by a long shot - either by the hours or even days.

Instead of setting arbitrary number of hours, I found that what worked best for me was to simply let my productivity flow. That I actually do more and accomplish more when I stop worrying about time itself - that I give my work however long it needs to get done and then call it a day.

This has allowed me to not be stressed that I never feel like I don't have enough time. Because in reality, time is relative. Time is something that I assign meaning to. If I simply focus on my designation, my 10 year plan, all I need to do is to simply work hard each day and that'll be good enough for me.

Right now the only thing that makes me feel like I don't have enough time, is when I actually waste them doing nothing meaningful. Having struggled with procrastination all my life, I've come to find out that I am not an innate workaholic. It doesn't come natural to me to want to do the work and that is what is causing me to feel like time is slipping away from me sometimes. That is something I have to continuously work on.

With regards to what you can learn from this - instead of racing against time to complete something, let the work flow out of you like water. Get into a state where productivity oozes out of you. Use a time tracking app to measure the amount of time that you have spent on working. Decide how much time you are willing to set aside to do your work and commit to that time. If 8 hours is the ideal, ensure that you clock those 8 hours and then end the day proud of yourself that you had already done what you set out to do at the start of the day. Never feel like you must do more and never beat yourself up for it. Be nicer to yourself as life is already hard enough as it is.

Another tip that I can recommend that has worked for me is to set a list of the top 3 things you want to do at the start of your day. Instead of the 10 that I did previously that caused me so much stress and anxiety, I have found that 3 is the ideal number of things that will bring us the most satisfaction and the least overwhelm when completing. If we are not able to complete those 3 big tasks, at least maybe we have done 1 or 2. We won't beat ourselves that we hadn't done those other 8 things at the back.

If on the other hand we have successfully completed all those 3 things by mid-day, we may choose to add another 3 items on our list. That way the carrot is never too far away and it is easily attainable should we want to add more.

So I challenge each and everyone of you to look into your day with a new set of lens. Set your intentions right at the start of each day and focus on productivity on a focused set of 3 items. Let the work flow out of you and let the task complete its course naturally without rushing. Remember that it will take as long as it takes and you will only bring yourself more stress if you set a deadline on it. Use it only as a tool for motivation but nothing else if you must set a deadline. Don't be too hard on yourself. Focus on the journey and don't be overly stressed out by feeling that you're always racing against time.

Chapter 12:

How to Learn Faster

Remember the saying, "You are never too old to learn something new"? Believe me, it's not true in any way you understood it.

The most reliable time to learn something new was the time when you were growing up. That was the time when your brain was in its most hyperactive state and could absorb anything you had thrown at it.

You can still learn, but you would have to change your approach to learning.

You won't learn everything, because you don't like everything going on around you. You naturally have an ego to please. So what can you do to boost your learning? Let's simplify the process. When you decide to learn something, take a moment and ask yourself this; "Will this thing make my life better? Will this fulfill my dreams? Will I benefit from it?".

If you can answer all these questions in a positive, you will pounce on the thing and you won't find anyone more motivated than you.

Learning is your brain's capability to process things constructively. If you pick up a career, you won't find it hard to flourish if you are genuinely interested in that particular skill.

Whether it be sports, singing, entrepreneurship, cooking, writing, or anything you want to pursue. Just ask yourself, can you use it to increase your creativity, your passion, your satisfaction. If you can, you will start learning it as if you knew it all along.

Your next step to learning faster would be to improve and excel at what you already have. How can you do that? It's simple yet again!

Ask yourself another question, that; "Why must I do this? Why do I need this?" if you get to answer that, you will find the fastest and effective way to the top yourself without any coaching. Why will this happen on its own? Because now you have found a purpose for your craft and the destination is clear as the bright sun in the sky.

The last but the most important thing to have a head start on your journey of learning is the simplest of them all, but the hardest to opt for. The most important step is to start working towards things.

The flow of learning is from Head to Heart to Hands. You have thought of the things you want to do in your brain. Then you asked your heart if it satisfied you. Now it's time to put your hands to work.

You never learn until you get the chance to experience the world yourself. When you go through a certain event, your brain starts to process the outcomes that could have been, and your heart tells you to give it one more try. Here is the deciding moment. If you listen to your heart right away, you will get on a path of learning that you have never seen before.

What remains now is your will to do what you have decided. And when you get going, you will find the most useful resources immediately. Use your instincts and capitalize your time. Capture every chance with sheer will and belief as if this is your final moment for your dreams to come true.

It doesn't matter if you are not the ace in the pack, it doesn't matter if you are not in your peak physical shape, it doesn't matter if you don't have the money yet. You will someday get all those things only if you had the right skills and the right moment.

For all you know, this moment right now is the most worth it moment. So don't go fishing in other tanks when you have your own aquarium. That aquarium is your body, mind, and soul. All you need is to dive deep with sheer determination and the stars are your limit.

Chapter 13:

Showing Up

Today we are going to talk about the simple concept of "Showing Up". And this is going to touch on the topic of motivation as well.

You see for many of us who struggle with laziness and a lack of willpower, we wait for inspiration to strike, or the perfect storm of feeling good and motivated before we make the effort to hit the hit or start taking action on the task that we have been putting off. We think that we need to be all pumped up and excited before doing anything, but many a times, these feelings are few and they rarely come when we expect them to.

There are days where I would plan a gym session only to cancel because I didn't feel like it. And there are times when I would plan a meetup with my friends only to feel lazy at the last second and cancelling. And there are also times when I plan to work at a particular cafe but decided against it because I was too tired.

All these moments where I lacked the willpower to get things started or keeping to my word only made my future commitments even more vulnerable to default. As i was giving in to my desires to be lazy, the next time it came around the excuses became easier and easier to justify. And that only led to a less favourable outcome with regards to my mental, physical, and emotional health. I was spiraling to a life of mediocrity every time i let my inner demon win.

This all changed when I came across an article that said that all you needed to do was to show up for your activity, even if u didn't want to. Just to do a quick 5 min session rather than a long 1 hour session that i would normally have planned out. Or to simply just get to the desk to work for 15mins rather than the 5 hours I would normally have set aside time to do.

I found that by the simple act of showing up for my activity, I had given myself the best possible chance to fulfilling that promise to myself. At the gym, one rep turned into 10 reps, and 5 mins of workout turned into a 2 hour one as i told myself you can do one more, and one more after that. And as I watched people workout around me, i felt motivated to put in more effort in my workout as well. This simple change made it easier for me to simply show up the next day at the gym and let the process play out on its own once again. The same principle came to work and play. I realised that all i needed to do was to get out of the house and the rest would take care of itself. To show up at my desk and gym, no matter how late I may be, that at least when I am there, I will begin the task one way or another.

I challenge each and everyone of you to give it a try. If you find the task that you dread to be too daunting, that Instead of setting a specific time that you need to spend on it, that you simply just show up. And let your body dictate how much time you should indeed spend on that activity.

Be it 5 mins or 5 hours. I have found that once I start something that it takes a lot of energy for me to stop. It is like a moving train or car, that once u get going you will most probably go till you can't go no more. Then you slowly grind to a halt and show up for the next activity.

I hope you have learned something today and I wish you all the best in getting your stuff done ASAP. Take care and i'll see you in the next one.

Chapter 14:

Fight Is The Reward

There are times in our lives when we feel blocked out. When we feel the darkness coming in. When we see the sun going down and seemingly never coming back up. When the winds feel tougher and everything coming in your way puts you down like a storm.

No matter how big and how defiant you get, life will always find a new way to knock you down.

You will often find yourself in a place where you have nowhere to go, but straight. And that straight path isn't always the easiest too. It has all these ridges and peaks or a long ditch. So you finally come to realize that the only way out is a challenge itself and you can't bow out because there is no other way around.

I want you to understand the concept of fight and struggle. The success stories and breakthroughs we all hear are mostly just 2 parts; its 90% work and 10% fight.

We all work and we all work hard. But the defining moment of our journey is the final fight we go through.

The work we put in gets us to the bottom of the final barrier but the effort we need to summit the peak is the fight we put in and finally get the breakthrough. But fighting isn't easy. It is the hardest part of your journey to success.

The fight you need to put in isn't just the Xs and O's. The true fight is your mental toughness. It's your sheer will to keep going and keep pushing because you are just around the corner for the ultimate success.

You are just on the verge of finding the best reward of your life. You are on the cusp of seeing and enjoying your happiest moments. Because you have finally found your dreams and you have finally fulfilled your purpose in life.

Now is the time to rise and give up the feeling of giving up. Now is the time to get on top of your challenges. Now is the time to sweat and get over that pain.

This is the moment you need to be at your best. This is the time you need your A-game. This is the time to defy all odds and go all in. Because the finals moments need the final straw of strength and effort in your body.

Make a decision and become your own light. Believe in yourself like you have never before and you will never look back.

So if you ask me again why is fighting worth it. It's because your attitude makes you win long before you have even set the foot in the battleground. It's your will to keep going that makes you stand out even before getting into the spotlight.

You don't win a fight when you fight, you win a fight before the fight even begins. Your ultimate reward is the collection of all your efforts and resilience.

Chapter 15:

There's No Time for Regrets

Regret. Guilt. Shame.

These are three of the darkest emotions any human will ever experience. We all feel these things at different points in our lives, especially after making a "bad" decision. There are certain situations some of us would rewind (or delete) if we could. The reality is, however, there is an infinite number of reasons we should never regret any of the decisions we make in our lives.

Here are 7 of them:

1. Every decision allows you to take credit for creating your own life.

Decisions are not always the result of thoughtful contemplation. Some of them are made on impulse alone. Regardless of the decision, when you made it, it was something you wanted, or you would not have done it (unless someone was pointing a gun at your head).

Be willing to own the decisions you make. Be accountable for them. Take responsibility and accept them.

2. By making any decision involving your heart, you have the chance to create more love in the world by spreading yours.

Your love is a gift.

Once you decide to love, do it without reservation. By fully giving of yourself, you expand your ability to express and receive love. You have added to the goodness of our universe by revealing your heart to it.

3. By experiencing the disappointment that might come with a decision's outcome, you can propel yourself to a new level of emotional evolution.

You aren't doing yourself any favors when you try to save yourself from disappointment. Disappointment provides you with an opportunity to redefine your experiences in life. By refining your reframing skills, you increase your resilience.

4. "Bad" decisions are your opportunity to master the art of self-forgiveness.

When you make a "bad" decision, *you* are the person who is usually the hardest on yourself. Before you can accept the consequences of your decision and move on, you must forgive yourself. You won't always make perfect choices in your life. Acknowledge the beauty in your human imperfection, then move forward and on.

5. Because of the occasional misstep, you enable yourself to live a Technicolor life.

Anger. Joy. Sadness.

These emotions add pigment to your life. Without these things, you would feel soulless. Your life would be black and white.

Make your decisions with gusto. Breathe with fire. You are here to live in color.

6. Your ability to make a decision is an opportunity to exercise the freedom that is your birthright.

How would you feel if you had no say in those decisions concerning your life? Would you feel powerless? Restricted? Suffocated?

Now, focus on what it feels like to make the decisions you want to make. What do you feel? Freedom? Liberty? Independence?

What feelings do you *want* to feel?

Freedom. Liberty. Independence.

As luck would have it, the freedom you want is yours. Be thankful for it in every decision you make, "good" or "bad."

7. When you decide to result in ugly aftermath, you refine what you *do* want in your life.

It's often impossible to know what you want until you experience what you don't want. With every decision, you will experience consequences.

Use those outcomes as a jumping-off point to something different (and better) in your future.

Chapter 16:

Why You Are Setting The Wrong Goals

Ever wondered why you are not getting any closer to your goals? Why you keep failing despite having all that effort? Why does someone else seem to be more successful?

Here are some thoughts for you to ponder.

You may have a good set of skills and all the eligibility criteria anyone else has. But you are not yet in the same spot you wished some years ago. Maybe it is not happening for your right now, because your approach to those goals is not correct. Or, maybe your goals are wrong altogether.

Let's say you had a goal to be someone or achieve something someday. But you never had any idea how to! So you started asking why am I not getting the success that I deserve, but never asked yourself, how can I get to that success.

So you might think that you have the right goals to achieve something. But the reality is, that you never had the right goals.

You should have set a single goal a single day. A single goal that you can achieve in a day will help you get on the right train at the right time with a limited effort.

You shouldn't think of the future itself, but the goal that you might achieve someday. Once you have that goal in mind, you shouldn't need a constant reminder every day just to create a scenario of depression and restlessness that won't help you rather strain unnecessary energy.

Once you have the final goal, put it aside and work towards the small goals that you can achieve in real-time with actual small efforts.

Once you have a grasp of these goals, you will find the next goal yourself; a goal that you might have never thought of before.

Just say you want to lose weight and you want to get to your ideal BMI someday. This is a valid and reasonable Goal to achieve. This might prolong your life and increase your self-worth. So you should have a set of regular goals that ultimately lead you to the final goal.

So you want to lose weight, start by reducing fats and carbs in your next meal, and the one after that and the next one.

It will be hard the first time. Maybe the same at the second time. But when you have envisioned the ultimate goal, you will be content with the healthier alternates as well.

Add 5 minutes of exercise the next day, along with the goals of the previous day. You will be reluctant to do it the first time, but when you see the sweat dripping from your chin, you will see your healthier self in each drop.

Every goal has its process. No matter how much you avoid the process, you will always find yourself at the mercy of mother nature, and nature has always a plan for execution.

Now it's your decision whether to be a part of that process or go down in history with a blank face with no name.

You will always find a way to cheat, but to cheat is another ten steps away from your penultimate goal.

Make it your goal to resist every temptation that makes your day no different than the previous one. Live your life on One day, Monday, Change day principle and you will always find yourself closer to your salvation.

The process of change is mundane. In fact, the process of everything in life is mundane. You have to apply certain steps and procedures for even doing the most basic tasks in your daily life.

Stop procrastinating because you are not fooling anyone else, just yourself. And if you keep fooling yourself, you will be the worst failure in the books of history.

Chapter 17:
The Power of Breathing To Reset Your Mind

Breathing is something we often take for granted. The breath is always there where we notice or not, keeping us going, and keeping us alive. Without our breath, our hearts will not have enough oxygen and we will die a very agonising death. Yet many of us forget to take the time out of the day to utilise this powerful tool of breathing mindfully to reset our focus, and to calm ourselves down in times of stress and anxiety.

Throughout the way, we are bombarded with things. Work stuff, people stuff, family stuff, and our minds and hearts begin racing and stay elevated throughout the day. Induced by stress hormones, we find ourselves full of cluttered thoughts and our productivity and focus drops as a result. Without clearing all these negative emotions that are bottled up inside us, we may find ourselves stressed out and unable to relax throughout the day, and even at night as we try to go to sleep.

This is where the power of conscious breathing comes into play. We all have the power and choice to take 30 seconds out of our day each time we feel that we need to settle down our emotions and clear our head.

Everytime you feel like things are getting out of control, simply stop whatever you are doing, close your eyes, and focus on breathing through our noise. Notice the breath that goes in and out of your nostrils as you inhale and exhale deeply.

By redirecting our focus to our breaths, we momentarily stop our automatic thoughts and are forced to direct attention to each intentional inhalation and exhalation. This conscious awareness to our breath serves to calm our nerves in times of volatility. If you don't believe it, try it for yourselves right now.

This technique has worked for me time and time again. Everytime i catch myself feeling distracted or unhappy, i would stop whatever i was doing, put on my noise cancelling earphones with the music turned off, and to just sit in complete silence as i focused on my breath. After about a minute or two, i find myself with a clearer head. A cleanse of sorts. And then i would attend to whatever task i was doing before.

This takes practice and awareness to be able to do consistently whenever negative emotions rise up. If you feel something is amiss 10x a day, you can carve out 10x of these deep breathing exercises each day as well. Try it and let me know your results.

Chapter 18:

10 Habits of Taylor Swift

Well-versed pop star isn't the only description for the "American Sweetheart" Taylor Swift- She's a woman with many talents and abilities. As a world-famous singer-songwriter, accomplished businesswoman, and fitness guru, Swift has risen to become one of the world's most renowned celebrities.

She signed her first record deal at the age of 15, has been nominated for over 500 awards, has won 324, and has sold over 50 million albums. Such success did not simply land to her automatically. As per the new Netflix documentary Miss Americana, Swift's growth is a journey of countless disappointing and challenging life and career lessons.

Here are 10 habits of Taylor Swift that can enrich your life and career path.

1. Certainty

Getting to where you want to be in life credits a clear vision. With a sense of clarity, you can pave the way to reach that destination.

Since the day she started her career in music, Taylor Swift has been clear on what she wanted. From the very young age she has served to steer her decision making, and enjoyed every bit of it.

2. Focus on the Brighter Side

Taylor Swift has had a share of public scandals, tabloids exploitation, and people who aimed at tarnishing her name with controversy. It is irrelevant whether they are justified or not, she continues to produce and thrive in her positive space. Just like Taylor Swift, develop an urge to always working past the ruins while strengthening your optimistic moods.

3. You Have No Control Over What Happens

The incident at 2009 VMAs with Kanye West fuelled Swift's desire to prove that her talent is undeniable. You'll learn from the Concert's footage performing her most critically acclaimed song, "All Too Well", that she's was not up to changing what people would eventually say about her but was only concerned with respecting her work ethic. Make your response to criticism a reflection of respect for your hustle!

4. Credit Your Success to Having a Niche

In the entertainment business, and with successful people like Taylor Swift, each one has their unique niche/speciality that sets them apart from everyone else. Major deeply on what makes you unique and what brought you there as your storyline is only for you to tell.

5. Courage Is the Secret to Longevity

Taylor went from being a trial for sexual assault, which she won the case, to her mother ailing from breast cancer and brain tumour to all the publicized stunts she had been through. Despite the challenges, she managed to produce indisputably remarkable projects. Just like Taylor, your confidence, resilience, brilliance, work ethic, and steadfast trust in your process will definitely garner appreciation and respect.

6. Own Your Power

Taylor Swift not only has power, but she also owns it. Following Scooter Braun and Scott Borchetta incident, Taylor was not scared to jeopardize her image or face the consequences of speaking up against something she honestly believed was unfair.

There are always risks to speaking out, but sitting silence may be far riskier. In some circumstances, being silent may endanger your opportunity to manage a project or receive a promotion or increase.

7. Develop Your Support System

Nurture your relationships if you'd like to gain more influence. Even though you are not on the same scale as Taylor Swift, maintained friendships influences your world. Listen to them if you want them to listen to you.

8. Follow Your Heroes

Taylor Swift started her profession at a young age. Her childhood was fraught with difficulties but had motivation from her idols, whom she followed their advice. If you adore someone who influences your life path, emulating two or three things from them pays off.

9. Be Influential

Taylor's success in the music industry has been her driving force in influencing other people. You don't have to have her numbers to be impactful. When you devote your time and energy to becoming productive, influential stats and metrics will follow you.

10. Maintain a Healthy Lifestyle

Being a celebrity doesn't mean that Swift's healthy lifestyle is about trendy diets and strange eating habits that dominates the entire Hollywood culture. According to PopSugar, Swift eats salads, nutritious sandwiches, yoghurt and hit the gym regularly during the week.

Conclusion

You don't have to be Taylor Swift, but you can learn from her. Increase your influence, cultivate your network, develop credibility, wield your authority, focus on positivity, resilience is vital, and feel free to stand your ground as you work on your uniqueness.

Chapter 19:

10 Habits of Dua Lipa

Dua Lipa is one of the world's enormous pop sensations in the history of the English pop music industry. Her music career broke through after releasing her single "Hotter than Hell" in 2016, and since then, she has been serving the world with hits after hits.

Dua has earned several Brit and Grammy Awards for the category of "Best New Artist" and her track, "Electricity" for "Best Dance Recording," and the "Best Solo British Female Artist," respectively. Additionally, she has won two MTV Europe Music Awards, one MTV Video Music Award, and an American Music Award. Her tracks are always top in both UK and US charts, and she is among the 2021"Time 100" list of the most influential people. How has she managed all this? Here are 10 habits of Dua Lipa.

1. Find Your Niche

Finding your niche is key to seeing where your strengths and weaknesses lie. Moreover, coming into terms with your abilities means taking them to step by step. Dua's first tracks didn't hit as much, but they helped Dua establish her synth-pop confidence. Later on, her singles, "Be the One, "Last Dance," and "Hotter Than Hell" defined her early work's whimsical tone and up-tempo drive and displayed her deep.

2. She's a Voracious Reader

Reading as a habit is essential for stimulation and enhancement of your intellect and creative ability. Dua Lipa is an ambitious person who appreciates a good book because she understands the value of reading in her creative career.

3. She's a Fashion Icon

Dua has not only earned a reputation through her award-winning records but also her flawless sense of style. Her dressing style revolves around two things: standing out and being confident. While her outfits will take you back to the '80s or '90s, you can't help but fall in love with her elegant mix of vintage and high-end brand pieces. If you look at her Instagram and red-carpet photos these days, you'll see a sartorial edge that matches her personality.

4. Confidence

Ever listened to "Blow Your Mind?" The song's lyrics and Dua's powerful voice will blow your mind off. It's a representation of confidence and self-esteem during challenging situations.

5. Self-Care Routine Is Key

Dua, through an interview, shared her daily self-care routine. She insisted on taking some time off your busy schedule to practice gratitude and spend time with your loved ones. Dua's self-care routine includes taking care of her vocal cords by steaming them, drinking tea, and remaining hydrated.

6. Bring a Killer Music Video With You

In this post-MTV era, an engaging music video is vital because they are part of why you'll hit a billion views on YouTube. Remember when Dua's "New Rules" came out? The song became Lipa's breakthrough when the video crossed one billion views a few months after its release, making her the youngest female artist to join the billion-view club.

7. Exhibit Your Personality

Your public presence as an artist differentiates you from a 'constant music producer in today's pop music. As "New Rules" took off for Dua, she introduced her endearingly sardonic online presence to millions of followers. There were self-deprecating tweets about her dance moves and spin-off memes to "New Rules," which frequently led to people demanding it more.

8. Improve Your Stage Performance

Outgrowing your insecurities demands some level of consistent practice. Dua toured non-stop from late 2016 through 2018, both as a headlining act and support with Bruno Mars and Coldplay. She had long been trolled for her dancing abilities during live performances and took such tour opportunities to advance as a dancer, live vocalist, and overall performance.

9. Predict the Trend With a Comeback Hit

Sometimes, what appears to be out of place will unpack your potential to create a trend. After Dua released "Don't Start Now," some disco-influenced songs like Doja Cat's "Say So," SZA and Justin Timberlake's "The Other Side," and Lady Gaga's "Stupid Love" made waves soared through a similar pop fixture.

10. Hit Again, With a Superb Sophomore Album

Dua's singles hit every niche of pop success since her career began, and her debut album, "Future Nostalgia," is everything you'd want to hear her at her peak. Dua's personality on this album is witty, sexy, vulnerable, and calm-a a goddess ready to start the party and a friend you want to gossip with.

Conclusion

Success is about doing what you're proud of. And just like Dua Lipa, determination and consistency are your tools to emerging as the best.

Chapter 20:

Stop Dwelling on Things

It's 5 p.m., the deadline for an important work project is at 6, and all you can think about is the fight you had with the next-door neighbor this morning. You're dwelling. "It's natural to look inward," but while most people pull out when they've done it enough, an overthinker will stay in the loop."

Ruminating regularly often leads to depression. So, if you're prone to obsessing (and you know who you are), try these tactics to head off the next full-tilt mental spin cycle...

1.Distract Yourself

Go and exercise, scrub the bathtub spotless, put on music and dance, do whatever engrosses you, and do it for at least 10 minutes. That's the minimum time required to break a cycle of thoughts.

2.Make a Date to Dwell

Tell yourself you can obsess all you want from 6 to 7 p.m., but until then, you're banned. "By 6 p.m., you'll probably be able to think things through more clearly,"

3. 3 Minutes of Mindfulness

For one minute, eyes closed, acknowledge all the thoughts going through your mind. For the next minute, just focus on your breathing. Spend the last minute expanding your awareness from your breath to your entire body. "Paying attention in this way gives you the room to see the questions you're asking yourself with less urgency and to reconsider them from a different perspective,"

4.The Best and Worst Scenarios

Ask yourself...

"What's the worst that could happen?" and "How would I cope?" Visualizing yourself handling the most extreme outcome should alleviate some anxiety. Then consider the likelihood that the worst will occur.

Next, imagine the best possible outcome; by this point, you'll be in a more positive frame of mind and better able to assess the situation more realistically.

5. Call a Friend

Ask a friend or relative to be your point person when your thoughts start to speed out of control.

6. Is it worth it?

If you find that your mind is fixated on a certain situation, ask yourself if the dwelling is worth your time.

'Ask yourself if looking over a certain situation will help you accept it, learn from it and find closure,' 'If the answer is no, you should make a conscious effort to shelve the issue and move on from it.'

7. Identify your anxiety trigger

There may be a pattern in your worries, and this means you can help identify potential causes and use practice preventative measures.

'For many of us, rumination will occur after a trigger, so it is important to identify what it is,' 'For example, if you have to give a presentation at work and the last one you didn't go to plan, this can cause rumination and anxiety.

Chapter 21:

7 Ways To Know When It's Time To Say Goodbye To The Past

Holding on to someone or something and fearing to let go is a problem that many of us will struggle with at some point or another. Be it a partner, career, or item, a history has been built around that and we find it hard to move on and leave this treasured piece behind.

Whether it be a 6months or 10 years, it can be hard for us to come to terms with letting go because we have invested so much time, energy, and soul, into it. Governed by emotions, we hold on to them even though it may no longer bring us happiness or joy.

Whatever the reasons are, here are 7 ways that can help you say goodbye to the past and invite better things into your life:

1. You've Drag things For Way Too Long

If it's a career that you're holding on to, you may feel that you've invested a lot of effort and energy in it, waiting for the time that you will get promoted. But the days come and go, months turn into years, and you find yourself a decade later wondering what happened. Letting things drag on is no way to live life. Time is precious and every moment we waste is a moment we can never get back.

2. You Know It's Time

People may tell us we're happy and that we should be so lucky to have this job or that person in our lives, but no one can hide the unhappiness that is festering within us. Deep down in our hearts, we understand ourselves more than any other people ever would. And we know, subconsciously, if it's time to move on and let go of the past. If you are unsure, do some soul-searching. Find a time to sit by yourself quietly, or go for a retreat on your own. Sort out your feelings and bring some clarity to yourself.

3. It No Longer Brings You Joy

With a person who we have spent so much energy being a relationship with over the years, it can be hard to come to terms with the reality that he or she no longer makes you feel happy or loved anymore. Being in a constant state of unhappiness is no way to live our lives. We have every power in us to make decisions that serves us rather than hinder us. Acknowledge and accept these feelings of unhappiness. Use it as fuel to make that important decision that you know you must make.

4. You Are Holding On Out of Fear

Many a times we hold out on ending that relationship with something because we live in a constant state of fear. Career-wise we may resign ourself to the fate that things are just the way it is and we are afraid that we may never find another job again. So we hold on to that false sense of security and just drag your feet till retirement. Relationship wise, we hold on to them because we fear we may never find someone else again. So we let fear keep us in these places, feeling more and more trapped in the process.

5.   You're Afraid of the Unknown

It is human nature to be afraid of the unknown. If we cannot see a clear path ahead, most of us would not dare to travel down that road. We don't know if the grass will be greener on the other side if we quit our jobs, and we don't know what the dating world will be like after being out of it for so long. We lose confidence in believing the unknown is a magical place and that wonderful things can happen there if we let ourselves take the leap of faith. That was how we got to where we were in the first place before we realized it no longer served us anymore.

6.   You're Ready For Change

This is similar to the second point about knowing it's time with one key difference - you know that you ready for a new phase of life. Having the urge to intact change in your life, you believe that you don't want to be stuck in whatever situation you are in anymore. You desperately want to make things better. Embrace these feelings and start taking strong action to force change to happen for you.

7.   You Know You Deserve Happiness

Happiness has to be earned. Happiness doesn't just happen to you. If you know you deserve to be happy, and that the current thing you are holding on to only brings you sorrow, it is time to let it go. Only when you let go of what's holding you down can you make room for better and brighter things. Putting yourself out there in the face of trials and errors is the only way you can find what you are truly looking for. Demand happiness and expect it to happen to you.

Conclusion
Saying goodbye to the past is not easy, and not everyone has the courage or strength to do it. You can either choose to live in fear, or you can choose to live a brave life. It is time to make that critical decision for yourself at this crossroad right now. Only one choice can bring you the life that you truly desire. So choose wisely.

Chapter 22:

Live A Long, Important Life

Do you think you are more capable to deal with the failure or the regret of not trying at all?

Are you living the life you want or the life everyone else wants for you?

Would you feel good spending your time on entertainment that might not last for long? Or would you feel good feeling like you are growing and have a better self of you to look at in the mirror?

Similarly, would like to live in the present or would you love to work for a better future?

Do you want money to dictate your life or do you want money to follow you where ever you go?

Would you prefer being tired or being broke?

Do you want to spend the rest of your life in this place where you and your parents were born? Or do you won't go around the world and find new possibilities in even the most remote places?

Would you rather risk it all or play it safe?

We are often presented with all these questions in our lifetime. Most people take these questions as a way to enter into your adulthood. The answers to these questions are meant to show you the actual meaning of life.

So what is Life? Life is not your parents, your work, your friends, your events, and your functions. It's within you and around you.

You should learn to live your life to the fullest. You should love to live your life for as long as you can with a happy body and a healthy mind.

A happy and healthy body and mind are important. Because you can only feel secure on a stable platform. You can only wish to stand on a platform where you know you can stay put for a long time.

There is nothing wrong with working eight or nine hours in your daily life. It's not unhealthy or anything. Working is what gives our life a purpose. Working is what keeps us active, moving, and motivated.

We have one life, and we have to make it matter. But the way we chose to do it is what matters the most. Our choices make us who we are rather than our actions.

The life we live is the epitome of our intentions and morals. We can be defined in a single word or a single phrase if we ever try. We don't need to analyze someone else, we just need to see ourselves in the mirror and we might be able to see right across the image.

The day we are able to do that, might be the day we have actually made a worthy human being of ourselves and have fulfilled our destiny.

If you are able to look at yourself and go through your whole life in the blink of an eye and cherish the memories as if you were right there at that moment. Believe me, you have had a long and important life to make you think of it all over again every day.

Chapter 23:

Dealing With Feelings of Overwhelm

Today we're going to talk about a topic that deals with feelings of stress and overwhelm, whether it be from your job or from your family and relationships. I hope that by the end of this video that you will be able to have strategies put in place to help you better cope with the feelings and manage your emotions much better. Hopefully you will also be able to eliminate the things in your life that brings your health into question. My job here is to help you as much as I can so let's begin.

First we have to identify the areas in your life that is bringing you unwanted stress and anxiety. I'm sure that if you think a little harder and dig a little deeper, you will be able to list out the things that are causing you to lose sleep over. The thought of that particular thing would trigger an immediate negative response in your body and only you know what they are.

So lets begin by just brainstorming and listing them down one by one. Take as much time as you need for this exercise. Next I want you to go through your list and arrange them according to which brings the most to the least stress. Now that you have this list, we can talk about the strategies that we can engage in to either reduce or eliminate this overwhelm.

Overwhelm can come from areas in our lives that we feel that we feel are out of control. We feel that we do not have a steady hand or the ability to manage this problem that it manifests into something that suddenly feels too big to handle. It could be something that you dread doing that you have procrastinated on, and that the problem just keeps growing bigger and bigger to the point where you don't even want to touch it. It could be from workloads being piled on top of you one after another by your bosses. It could be a project that you undertook that just maybe is too big for you to handle at your current level and expertise. It could be your family who is giving you additional problems that you have to deal with on top of your workload that is just driving you up the wall. Whatever the stresses are that contributes to your problem, know that they are valid, know that they are real and that they are normal.

Everyone goes through periods of their lives when things just all seem to happen at once. Whether it be having a new baby, a new promotion, a new career, starting a new chapter in life, it is usually those big changes in life that we face overwhelm due to the sudden and added workload that we are not used to. Overwhelm can cause us to lose sleep, lose appetite, gain weight, experience chronic stress, and all these negative aspects can surface in our bodies in ways that affect our health and wellness. When we see these triggers, it is time to make some changes.

We can start by slowing things down a little and carving out time for ourselves to be alone and to recharge. I believe great way for us to get in touch with ourselves is through yoga and meditation. While it might seem like fluff at first, I have personally tried it myself and it is in those moments of calm and relaxation that my head is truly clear. When I am actually able to hear my own thoughts and be aware of what is happening around me. During times we feel overwhelm, things can happen so fast that we lose track of who we are. And sometimes all we need to do is to bring back the attention to ourselves. Find a meditative yoga practice on audible or YouTube, or even Apple Music and Spotify if it is available. Let the teacher guide you through the practice. And just let yourself go for that 30mins or 1 hour that you choose to set aside for yourself. You will be amazed at how calm you will feel and how clear your goals will be if you do it on a regular basis.

With this clarify you may be able to make better decisions that hopefully helps you get through your rough periods that much easier. Whenever you find yourself feeling stress and overwhelm, just give yourself another 15mins to be calm and be guided through a short meditation practice.

The next thing we can do to help alleviate feelings of overwhelm is to practice slow and deep breathing. Focusing on the breath as been proven to reduce stress by triggering a physiological response in our body. We trick our brain into slowing down and focusing on one thing and one thing only. This trick can help to calm you in moments of deep anxiety when you feel the world is crashing down on you and you are not sure what to do. Just sit still for a moment and engage in this practice.

Now we have to address the elephant in the room which is what are the areas in your life that are triggering these responses from your body that is causing you to feel overwhelm. And is there any way we can eliminate these stressors from your life. Again as I have said many times before, if this thing you are doing is bringing you such immense dread and overwhelm, maybe it is time you simply walk away from it forever if that is an option. You have to ask yourself if what you are doing can justify putting your mental and physical state in jeopardy. Whether maybe the money is worth risking your health over, or whether this person is worth keeping in your life if he or she brings you much anguish. I always believe that life is too short to be filled with things that overwhelm us. A little stress is good for us but chronic and prolonged periods of exposure to this can in fact cause us to die sooner. As cortisol is constantly being pumped into your bloodstream it can have serious negative consequences for our physical health, not to mention our mental health in the form of depression.

Sometimes we have to tell ourselves it is okay to simply walk away when we have no other option. Something or someone else will turn up that is better for us if we put ourselves first.

So I urge all of you to take a hard look at the list you have created today. Which ones on those list have you been suffering for prolonged periods of time with seemingly no end to it? Could you eliminate it from your life or take a smaller role on it? Always remember that you are what you take on, and that you have the power to decide what you want in your life. I believe you know how to make the right decisions for yourself as well.

Chapter 24:

<u>Overcoming the Fear of Failure</u>

Stop it.

Stop whatever you are doing and take a moment to listen because you need to hear this...

Right now I want you to close your eyes and remember a time that you failed. I want you to remember how it made you feel. Remember the pain. Remember the guilt. Dig deep and remember the crushing weight of DISAPPOINTMENT that dragged you down to the depths of hell.

Do you feel it?! DO YOU REMEMBER THAT FEELING?! Good. Now get used to it - because you're gonna feel it again.

I need you to understand that failure is a part of life. In fact it's more than that. It's an essential part of life, of success! You think winners never failed? You think it's just you? Winners have failed more times than losers have ever TRIED!

People who succeed don't stop when they fail. They don't stop at ten, fifty or a hundred failures! They push through. They persevere. It doesn't matter how many times they get knocked down. They get right back up. Again. And again. And again. You know why? They don't fear failure.

Listen closely, because this will change your life. So long as you fear failure, you will never achieve success. You will never reach your dreams. Fearing failure is the only thing stopping you from becoming great. Greatness is a title reserved only for those who are willing to go head to head with failure - for those who face the fear of failure without hesitation! They look failure in the eye and say "I'll be damned if I let YOU sat and in my way!"

When they asked Michael Jordan how many shots he made, you know what he said? He told them they were nothing compared to how many he missed. Michael Jordan became the greatest basketball player of all time because he wasn't afraid to fail! What do you think would have happened if he had given up? If he had been scared to fail. He would never have become the legend that he did. He would have stayed a nobody - just like you.

Did that hurt? How did it make you feel? The pain. The guilt. The disappointment of knowing that so long as you fear failure YOU WILL BE A NOBODY. Your talent, your ability, the greatness within you! They will all die within you. If you aren't ready to accept that, then you need to make a change.

Get up. Get up from wherever you are hiding and face failure one on one. That fear is the only thing standing between you and success. You've got to get it through your head that this is it, the moment of truth. This is the time to decide who you are. Either you are a winner or a loser. If you can't look failure in the eye to achieve your dreams then you will never rise beyond mediocrity. But if you are a winner, now is the time to prove it. Forget mediocrity, you rise to the occasion. Failure is nothing more than one step closer to the greatness you desire. And if you can do that, if you can overcome the fear of failure... you can do anything.

Chapter 25:

Setting Too High Expectations

Today we're going to talk about the topic of setting too high expectations. Expectations about everything from work, to income, to colleagues, friends, partners, children, family. Hopefully by the end of this video I will be able to help you take things down a notch in some areas so that you don't always get disappointed when things don't turn out the way you expect it to.

Let's go one by one in each of these areas and hopefully we can address the points that you are actively engaged in at the moment.

Let's begin with work and career. Many of us have high expectations for how we want our work life to be. How we expect our companies and colleagues to behave and the culture that we are subjected to everyday. More often that not though, companies are in the business of profit-making and cutting costs. And our high expectations may not meet reality and we might end up getting let down. What I would recommend here is that we not set these expectations of our colleagues and bosses, but rather we should focus on how we can best navigate through this obstacle course that is put in front of us. We may want to focus instead on how we can handle ourselves and our workload. If however we find that we just can't shake off this expectations that we want from working in a company, maybe we want to look elsewhere to companies that have a work culture that suits our personality. Maybe one that is more vibrant and encourages freedom of expression.

Another area that we should address is setting high expectations of our partners and children. Remember that we are all human, and that every person is their own person. Your expectations of them may not be their expectations of themselves. When you impose such an ideal on them, it may be hard for them to live up to. Sure you should expect your partner to be there for you and for your children to behave a certain way. But beyond that everyone has their own personalities and their own thoughts and ideas. And what they want may not be in line with what we want for them. Many a times for Asian parents, we expect our kids to get good grades, get into good colleges, and maybe becoming a doctor or lawyer one day. But how many of us actually understand what our kids really want? How many of us actually listen to what our kids expect of themselves? Maybe they really want to be great at music, or a sport, or even finance. Who's to say what's actually right? We should learn to trust others and let go of some of our own expectations of them and let them become whoever they want to be.

The next area I want to talk about is simply setting too high expectations of yourself. Many times we have an ideal of who we want to be - how we want to look, how we want our bodies to look, and how we want our bank statement to look, amongst many others. The danger here is when we set unrealistic expectations as to when we expect these things to happen. Remember most things in life takes time to happen. The sooner you realise that you need more time to get there, the easier it will be on yourself. When we set unrealistic timelines, while it may seem ideal to rush through the process to get results fast, more often than not we are left disappointed when we don't hit them. We then get discouraged and may even feel like a failure or give up the whole process entirely. Wouldn't it be better if we could give ourselves more time for nature to work its magic? Assuming you follow the steps that you have laid out and the action plans you need to take, just stretch this timeline out a little farther to give yourself more breathing room. If you feel you are not progressing as fast as you had hoped, it is okay to seek help and to tweak your plans as they go along. Don't ever let your high expectations discourage you and always have faith and trust in the process even when it seems hard.

One final thing I want to talk about is how we can shift from setting too high expectations to one of setting far-out goals instead. There is a difference. Set goals that serve to motivate you and inspire you to do things rather than ones that are out of fear. When we say we expect something, we immediately set ourselves up for disappoint. However if we tell ourselves that we really want something, or that we want to achieve something that is of great importance to us, we shift to a goal-oriented mindset. One that is a lot healthier. We no longer fear the deadline creeping up on us. We instead continually work on getting there no matter how long it takes. That we tell ourselves we will get there no matter what, no matter how long. The key is to keep at it consistently and never give up.

Having the desire to work at an Apple store as a retail specialist, I never let myself say that I expect apple to hire me by a certain time otherwise I am never pursuing the job ever again. Rather I tell myself that being an Apple specialist is my dream job and that I will keep applying and trying and constantly trying to improve myself until Apple has no choice but to hire me one day. A deadline no longer bothers me anymore. While I wait for them to take me in, I will continue to pursue other areas of interest that will also move my life forward rather than letting circumstances dictate my actions. I know that I am always in control of my own ship and that I will get whatever I put my mind to eventually if I try hard enough.

So with that I challenge each and every one of you to be nicer to yourselves. Lower your lofty expectations and focus on the journey instead of the deadline. Learn to appreciate the little things around you and not let your ego get in the way.

Chapter 26:

How To Crush Your Goals This Quarter

Some people find it very hard to achieve their goals, but luckily, there is a method waiting to be used. The quarter method divides the year into four parts of 90-days; for each part, you set some goals to crush. The rest of the year has gone, and so have the three quarters; now it is time to prepare for the fourth quarter. 1st October is one of the most critical days in the life of a person who sets his goals according to the quarter. It is the benchmark representing the close of the third quarter and the beginning of the fourth quarter. It is the day when you set new goals for the upcoming three months; if somehow your third-quarter dreams were not crushed, then you can stage a comeback so you wouldn't be left behind forever. But how to achieve your fourth-quarter goals?

1st October may bring the start of a quarter, but it also ends another quarter; it is the day when you focus on your results. Have you achieved the goals you set for the third quarter? If not, then prepare yourself to hear the hard truth. Your results reflect your self-esteem; if you believe in yourself, then you would achieve your goals. If you are not satisfied with your results, think, is this what you had in mind? If no, then having small visions can never lead to a more significant impact. Limiting beliefs will never give you more than minor and unimpressive results. Your results tell you about your passion for your work; if you are not passionate about your work, you would have poor outcomes. We all have heard the famous saying, " work in silence and let your success make the noise," but what does this mean? It means that your results will tell everyone about your hard work. If your results are not satisfactory, you know that the problem is your behavior towards your work.

When setting goals for the future, one needs to accept the facts; what went wrong that put you off the track? The year is 75% complete, and if you still haven't crushed your goals, you need to accept that it is your fault. If you blame these failures on your upbringing, your education, or any other factor than yourself, then you are simply fooling yourself because it is all dependent on you. When you don't achieve what you wanted to in nine months, you must have figured the problem; it can be any bad habit you are not willing to give up or the strategies you are implying. If you pretend your habits, attitude, and approach are just fine, you are just fooling yourself, not anyone else. This benchmark is the best time to change the old bad habits and try forming some new strategies.

To finish the year with solid results, you need to get serious; the days of dissatisfied results are gone, now it is time to shine some light on your soul and determine what you are doing wrong, what habits are working in your favor, and which ones are not. Then you can decide which habits to give up on, which habits to improve, and which ones to keep. Once you have sorted this out, prioritize your goals and set some challenging destinations to avoid getting bored or feeling uninterested. When setting deadlines, try to set enforceable deadlines.

Confusion can lead to poor results, so sit back and think about the goals that I should not pursue. This is called understanding goal competition; the goals you set are competing for your time. Actual peak performance comes from understanding which goals to pursue and which not to seek. And when you complete a plan, don't just rush into the process of crushing the next goal; allow yourself to celebrate your win and feel the happiness of the goal finally getting destroyed by you.

Chapter 27:

How To Deal With Feelings of Unworthiness

Today we're going to talk about a topic that I hope none of you struggle with. But if you do, I hope to bring some light into your life today. Because i too have had to deal with such feelings before, as recently as a year ago actually.

So before we get into the solutions, we must first understand where these feelings of unworthiness comes form. And we must be aware of them before we can make changes in our lives that brings us out of that state of mind.

Let's start with my life, maybe you will understand the kinds of struggles that I had gone through that led me to feeling unworthy.

Just about 3 years ago, I started my entrepreneurial journey, a journey that was full of excitement and curiousity. After being through a couple of internships at a company, i knew the corporate life wasn't really my thing, and i set out on my own path to making money online... To see if i could find a way to have an income without having to work a 9-5 job. The start was rough as I had no experience whatsoever. But over time i started to find a bit of footing and I made some decent income here and there that would sustain my livelihood for a while. As I was starting to see some success, my "world" came crashing down as something happened with the small business that I had spent almost 3 years building up. And suddenly my income was gone. And I realized I had nothing to show for my 3 years of work. It left me feeling incredibly depressed... Although it doesnt sound like the end of the world to many of you, i felt like i had been set back many years behind my peers who were by then already steadily climbing up the corporate ladder. Feelings that I had made a grave mistake in terms of career choice started creeping up on me. As I tried to figure out what to do with my life, I couldn't help but compare my income to the income that my friends were making. And I felt did feel worthless, and inferior. And I started questioning my whole journey and life choices up till that point.

I started wondering if I was ever going to climb my way back up again, if I would ever figure out how these things actually worked, and all those negative thoughts came day in and out. Eating me alive inside.

It was only after I had done some introspection did I finally started to learn to love myself. And to learn that my journey is unique and mine alone. That I didn't need to, and must not, compare myself to others, did i really start to feel worthy again. I started to believe in my own path, and I felt proud that I had dared to try something that most of my peers were afraid to even try. I found new qualities in myself that I didn't knew I had and I started to forge a new path for myself in my own entrepreneurial journey. Eventually my experience making money online helped me claw my way back up the income ladder, and I have never looked backed since.

For me personally, the one thing that I could take away from my own experience with unworthiness, is to not compare yourself with others. You will never be happy comparing with your peers on income, relationship status, number of friends, number of followers on social media, and all that random things. If you always look at your friends in that way, you will always feel inferior because there will always be someone better than you. Sure you can look to them for inspiration and tips, but never feel that they are superior to you in anyway.. because you are unique in your own beautiful way. You should focus on your own journey and how you can be a better version of yourself. Your peers might have different sets of skills, talents, and expertise, that helped them excel in their fields, but you have your own talents too that you should exploit. You never know what you can achieve until you truly believe in yourself and fully utilise your potential.

For you, your struggle with unworthiness could stem from the way your parents compare you to your siblings, or feeling hopeless trying to find love in this cruel world, or being rejected by companies in your Job applications, or rejection by a potential suitor. These are all valid things that can bring us down. But never let these people tell you what you can or cannot do. Prove to them that you are worthy by constantly improving yourself, mentally, physically, health wise, being emotionally resilient, grow your wisdom, and always love yourself. People cannot love you if you do not love yourself first. That is a quote that i believe very deeply.

No amount of validation from external sources can match the love that I decide to give to myself first.

If you find yourself in situations where you are being bombarded with negativity, whether it be from friends or family, i suggest you take a step back from these people. Find a community where your achievements are celebrated and appreciated, and where you can also offer the same amount of encouragement to others. Join meetup groups in your area with people of similar interests and just enjoy the journey. You will get there eventually if you believe in yourself.

So I challenge each and every one of you to always choose yourself first, look at your own journey as a unique path, different from everybody else, follow your dreams, take action, and never give up. That is the only way to prove to yourself and to the world that you are the most worthy person on the planet.

Chapter 28:

Avoid The Dreaded Burnout

Do you often lack the energy to get on with any new task and feel sluggish throughout most of your day? Do you feel the burden of work that keeps getting pilled up each day?

I know we all try our best to manage everything on our hands and try to bring out the best in us. But while doing so, we engage in too many things and ultimately they take their toll.

It is becoming easier and easier every day where people have more work than ever on their hands. And their sole motive throughout life becomes, to find more and better ways of earning a better living. To find more things to be good and successful at.

We all have things on our hands to complete but let me tell you one thing. You won't be able to continue much longer if you keep with this burnout and exhaustion.

Our body is an engine and it needs a way of cooling down and tuning. So what's the first step you need to reduce burnout? You need to get the right amount of sleep.

There is this myth that you sleep one-third of your life so you don't need an 8-hour sleep. You can easily do the same with four hours and use the other four for more work. Trust me, this is not a myth, it is a misconception about proven research. Your body organs deserve at least half the time of what they spend serving us.

We can refresh and better our focus and cognitive skills once we have a good night's sleep full of dreams.

Another thing that most of us avoid doing is to say No to anyone anytime. The thing is that we don't have any obligation to anyone unless we are bound by a contract of blood or law to do or say anything that anyone tells us to do. The more we feel obligated to anyone, the more we try to do to impress that person or entity with our efforts and conduct.

This attitude isn't healthy for any relation. Excess of anything has never brought any good to anyone. So don't give up everything on just one thing. Instead, try to devise a balance between things. Over-commitment is never a good idea.

The third and final thing I want you to do is to give up on certain things at certain times. You don't need to carry your phone or laptop with you all day. This only creates a distraction even when you don't need to be in that environment.

You don't need to train your subconscious to be always alert on your emails and notifications or any incoming calls all day long. But sometimes you just need to give up on these things and zone out of your repetitive daily life.

Doing your best doesn't always mean giving yourself all out. Sometimes the best productive thing you can do is to relax. And that, my friends, can help you climb every mountain without ever getting tired of trying t do the same trail.

Chapter 29:

Planning Ahead

The topic that are going to discuss today is probably one that is probably not going to apply to everybody, especially for those who have already settled down with a house, wife, kids, a stable career, and so on. But i still believe that we can all still learn something from it. And that is to think about planning ahead. Or rather, thinking long term.

You see, for the majority of us, we are trained to see maybe 1 to 2 years ahead in our lives. Being trained to do so in school, we tend to look towards our next grade, one year at a time. And this system has ingrained in us that we find it hard to see what might and could happen 2 or 3 years down the road.

Whilst there is nothing wrong with living life one year at a time, we tend to fall into a short term view of what we can achieve. We tell ourselves we must learn a new instrument within 1 year and be great at it, or we must get this job in one year and become the head of department, or we must find our partner and get married within a short amount of time. However, life does not really work that way, and things actually do take much longer, and we do actually need more time to grow these small little shoots into big trees.

We fail to see that we might have to give ourselves a longer runway time of maybe 3-5 or even 10 years before we can become masters in a new instrument, job, relationship, or even friendships. Rome isn't built in a day and we shouldn't expect to see results if we only allow ourselves 1 year to accomplish those tasks. Giving ourselves only 1 year to achieve the things we want can put unnecessary pressure on ourselves to expect results fast, when in reality no matter how much you think u think rushing can help you achieve results faster, you might end up burning yourself out instead.

For those short term planners, even myself. I have felt that at many stages in my life, i struggle to see the big picture. I struggle to see how much i can achieve in lets say 5 years if i only allowed myself that amount of time to become a master in whatever challenge i decide to take on. Even the greatest athletes take a longer term view to their career. They believe that if they practice hard each day, they might not expect to see results in the first year, but as their efforts compound, by the 5th year they would have already done so much practice that it is statistically impossible not to be good at it.

And when many of us fall into the trap of simply planning short term, our body reacts by trying to rush the process as well. We expect everything to be fast fast fast, and results to be now now now. And we set unrealistic goals that we cannot achieve and we beat ourselves up for it come December 31st.

Instead i believe many of us should plan ahead by giving ourselves a minimum of 2.5 years in whatever task we set to achieve, be it an income goal, a fitness goal, or a relationship goal. 2.5 years is definitely much more manageable and it gives us enough room to breathe so that we don't stress ourselves out unnecessarily. If you feel like being kinder to yourself, you might even give yourselves up to 5 years.

And again the key to achieving success with proper long term planning is Consistency. If you haven't watched my video on consistency do check it out as i believe it is one of the most important videos that I have ever created.

I believe that with a run time of 5 years and consistency in putting the hours every single day, whether it is an hour or 10 hours, that by the end of it, there is no goal that you cannot achieve. And we should play an even longer game of 10 years or so. Because many of the changes we want to make in life should be permanent and sustainable. Not a one off thing.

So I challenge each and everyone of you today to not only plan ahead, but to think ahead of the longevity of the path that you have set for yourself. There is no point rushing through life and missing all the incredible sights along the way. I am sure you will be a much happier person for it.

I hope you learned something today, take care and I'll see you in the next one.

Chapter 30:

Happy People Don't Sweat the Small Stuff.

Stress follows a peculiar principle: when life hits us with big crises—the death of a loved one or a job loss—we somehow find the inner strength to endure these upheavals in due course. It's the little things that drive us insane day after day—traffic congestion, awful service at a restaurant, an overbearing coworker taking credit for your work, meddling in-laws, for example.

It's all too easy to get caught up in the many irritations of life. We overdramatize and overreact to life's myriad tribulations. Under the direct influence of anguish, our minds are bewildered, and we feel disoriented. This creates stress, which makes the problems more difficult to deal with.

The central thesis of psychotherapist Richard Carlson's bestselling *Doesn't Sweat The Small Stuff... And It's All Small Stuff* (1997) is this: to deal with angst or anger, we need not some upbeat self-help prescriptions for changing ourselves, but simply a measure of perspective.

Perspective helps us understand that there's an art to understand what we should let go of and what we should concern ourselves with. It is important to focus our efforts on the important stuff and not waste time on insignificant and incidental things.

I've previously written about my favorite 5-5-5 technique for gaining perspective and guarding myself against anger erupting: I remove myself from the offending environment and contemplate if whatever I'm getting worked up over is of importance. I ask myself, "Will this matter in 5 days? Will this matter in 5 months? Will this matter in 5 years?"

Carlson stresses that there's always a vantage point from which even the biggest stressor can be effectively dealt with. The challenge is to keep making that shift in perspective. When we achieve that "wise-person-in-me" perspective, our problems seem more controllable and our lives more peaceful.

Carlson's prescriptions aren't uncommon—we can learn to be more patient, compassionate, generous, grateful, and kind, all of which will improve the way we feel about ourselves and how other people feel when they are around us.

Some of Carlson's 100 recommendations are trite and banal—for example, "make peace with imperfection," "think of your problems as potential teachers," "remember that when you die, your 'in-basket' won't be empty," and "do one thing at a time." Others are more informative:

- Let others have the glory
- Let others be "right" most of the time
- Become aware of your moods, and don't allow yourself to be fooled by the low ones
- Look beyond behavior
- Every day, tell at least one person something you like, admire, or appreciate about them.
- Argue for your limitations, and they're yours
- Resist the urge to criticize
- Read articles and books with entirely different points of view from your own and try to learn something.

Chapter 31:

How To Worry Less

How many of you worry about little things that affect the way you go about your day? That when you're out with your friends having a good time or just carrying out your daily activities, when out of nowhere a sudden burst of sadness enters your heart and mind and immediately you start to think about the worries and troubles you are facing. It is like you're fighting to stay positive and just enjoy your day but your mind just won't let you. It becomes a tug of war or a battle to see who wins?

How many of you also lose sleep because your mind starts racing at bedtime and you're flooded with sad feelings of uncertainty, despair, worthlessness or other negative emotions that when you wake up, that feeling of dread immediately overwhelms you and you just feel like life is too difficult and you just dont want to get out of bed.

Well If you have felt those things or are feeling those things right now, I want to tell you you're not alone. Because I too struggle with those feelings or emotions on a regular basis.

At the time of writing this, I was faced with many uncertainties in life. My business had just ran into some problems, my stocks weren't doing well, I had lost money, my bank account was telling me I wasn't good enough, but most importantly, i had lost confidence. I had lost the ability to face each day with confidence that things will get better. I felt that i was worthless and that bad things will always happen to me. I kept seeing the negative side of things and it took a great deal of emotional toll on me. It wasn't like i chose to think and feel these things, but they just came into my mind whenever they liked. It was like a parasite feeding off my negative energy and thriving on it, and weakening me at the same time.

Now your struggles may be different. You may have a totally different set of circumstances and struggles that you're facing, but the underlying issue is the same. We all go through times of despair, worry, frustration, and uncertainty. And it's totally normal and we shouldn't feel ashamed of it but to accept that it is a part of life and part of our reality.

But there are things we can do to minimise these worries and to shift to a healthier thought pattern that increases our ability to fight off these negative emotions.

I want to give you 5 actionable steps that you can take to worry less and be happier. And these steps are interlinked that can be carried out in fluid succession for the greatest benefit to you. But of course you can choose whichever ones speaks the most to you and it is more important that you are able to practice any one of these steps consistently rather than doing all 5 of them haphazardly. But I want to make sure I give you all the tools so that you can make the best decisions for yourself.

Try this with me right now as I go through these 5 steps and experience the benefit for yourself instead of waiting until something bad happens.

The very first step is simple. Just breathe. When a terrible feeling of sadness rushes into your body out of nowhere, take that as a cue to close your eyes, stop whatever you are doing, and take 5 deep breathes through your nose. Breathing into your chest and diaphragm. Deep breathing has the physiological benefit of calming your nerves and releasing tension in the body and it is a quick way to block out your negative thoughts. Pause the video if you need to do practice your deep breathing before we move on.

And as you deep breathe, begin the second step. Which is to practice gratefulness. Be grateful for what you already have instead of what you think u need to have to be happy. You could be grateful for your dog, your family, your friends, and whatever means the most to you. And if you cannot think of anything to be grateful for, just be grateful that you are even alive and walking on this earth today because that is special and amazing in its own right.

Next is to practice love and kindness to yourself. You are too special and too important to be so cruel to yourself. You deserve to be loved and you owe it to yourself to be kind and forgiving. Life is tough as it is, don't make it harder. If you don't believe in yourself, I believe in you and I believe in your worthiness as a person that you have a lot left to give.

The fourth step is to Live Everyday as if it were your last. Ask yourself, will you still want to spend your time worrying about things out of your control if it was your last day on earth? Will you be able to forgive yourself if you spent 23 out of the last 24 hours of your life worrying? Or will you choose to make the most out of the day by doing things that are meaningful and to practice love to your family, friends, and yourself?

Finally, I just want you to believe in yourself and Have hope that whatever actions you are taking now will bear fruition in the future. That they will not be in vain. That at the end of the day, you have done everything to the very best of your ability and you will have no regrets and you have left no stone unturned.

How do you feel now? Do you feel that it has helped at least a little or even a lot in shaping how you view things now? That you can shift your perspective and focus on the positives instead of the worries?

If it has worked for you today, I want to challenge you to consistently practice as many of these 5 steps throughout your daily lives every single day. When you feel a deep sadness coming over you, come back to this video if you need guidance, or practice these steps if you remember them on your own.

I wish you only good things and I hope that I have helped you that much more today. Thank you for your supporting me and this channel and if you find that I can do more for you, do subscribe to my channel and I'll see you in the next one. Take care.

Chapter 32:

Dealing With Difficult People

It is inevitable that people will rub us the wrong way as we go about our days. Dealing with such people requires a lot of patience and self-control, especially if they are persistent in their actions towards you over a lengthy period of time.

Difficult people are outside the realm of our control and hence we need to implement strategies to deal with negative emotions should they arise. If you encounter such people frequently, here are 7 ways that you can take back control of the situation.

2. Write Your Feelings Down Immediately
A lot of times we bottle up feelings when someone is rude or unpleasant to us. We may have an urge to respond but in the moment we choose not to. In those circumstances, the next best thing we can do is to write down our feelings either in our journals or in our smartphones as notes.

Writing our feelings down is a therapeutic way to cleanse our thoughts and negative energy. In writing we can say the things we wished we had said, and find out the reasons that made us feel uneasy in the first place. In writing we are also able to clearly identify the trigger points and could work backwards in managing our expectations and feelings around the person. If it is a rude customer, or a rude stranger, we may not be able to respond for fear or retaliation or for fear of losing our jobs. It is best those situations not to erupt in anger, but take the time to work through those emotions in writing.

3.   Tell The Person Directly What You Dislike About Their Attitude

If customer service and retail isn't your profession, or if it is not your boss, you may have the power to voice your opinion directly to the person who wronged you. If confrontation is something that you are comfortable with, don't hesitate to express to them why you are dissatisfied with their treatment or attitude towards you. You may also prefer to clear your head before coming back to confront the person and not let emotions escalate. A fight is the last thing we want out of this communication.

4.   Give An Honest Feedback Where Possible On Their Website

If physical confrontation is not your cup of tea, consider writing in a feedback online to express your dissatisfaction. We are usually able to write the most clear and precise account of the situation when we have time to process what went wrong. Instead of handling this confrontation ourselves, the Human Resources team would most likely deal with this person directly, saving you the trouble in the process. Make sure to give an accurate account of the situation and not exaggerate the contents to make the person look extremely in the wrong, although it can be tough to contain our emotions when we are so riled up.

5. Use this Energy To Fuel Your Fire

Sometimes, taking all these energy and intense emotions we feel may fuel our fire to work harder or to prove to others that we are not deserving of their hatred. Be careful though not to take things too far. Remember that ultimately you have the power to choose whether to let this person affect you. If you choose to accept these emotions, use them wisely.

6. Channel This Intense Emotion Into A Craft That Allows You To Release Unwanted Feelings

For those who have musical talents, we may use this negative experience to write a song about it while we are at the heights of our emotions. In those moments the feelings are usually intense, and we all know that emotions can sometimes produce the best works of art. If playing an instrument, writing an article, producing a movie clip, or crushing a sport is something that comes natural to us, we may channel and convert these emotions into masterpieces. Think Adele, Taylor Swift, and all the great songwriters of our generation as an example.

7. Learn To Grow Your Patience

Sometimes not saying anything at all could be the best course of action. Depending on the type of person you are, and the level of zen you have in you, you may not be so easily phased by negativity if you have very high control of your emotions. Through regular meditation and deep breathing, we can let go of these bad vibes that people send our way and just watch it vanish into a cloud of smoke. Regular yoga and meditation practices are good ways to train and grow your patience.

8.   Stand Up For Yourself

At the end of the day, you have to choose when and if you want to stand up for yourself if someone has truly wronged you. We can only be so patient and kind to someone before we snap. Never be afraid to speak your truth and defend yourself if you feel that you have been wrongfully judged. Difficult people make our lives unpleasant but it doesn't mean we should allow them to walk all over us without consequences. You have every right to fight for your rights, even if it means giving up something important in the process to defend it.

Chapter 33:

Putting Exercise First

In this topic we're going to talk about why you should consider putting exercise first above all else in your daily routine and the benefits that it can bring to your health and all other aspects of your life.

Many of us don't usually prioritise work as the most essential part of our day. We have work, family, kids, money, and a whole host of problems to worry about that exercise usually comes in dead last on the list of things to do. What we fail to realise is that exercise is the one thing that we might need most to keep us fit and healthy to take on the challenges that life throws at us each and every day.

I'm sure you all know the benefits of exercise. Doing it regularly can bring lots of benefits to your metabolism, alertness, energy, BMI, muscle mass, and so on. But what does it really mean?

Have you ever wondered why you are always feeling tired all the time? Or why you feel like you haven't really woken up yet when you're already sitting in front of your desk at the office?

You see, it is the time of your exercise that matters a lot too. A lot of successful CEOs and entrepreneurs actually make exercise the first thing they do when they wake up from bed. The reason is simple, it gets the body moving which in turns starts the engine that drives you out of lethargy and into an active physical state. As you move on a treadmill or do yoga early in the morning, your heart starts pumping faster which drives more blood into other areas of your body to wake you up.

And this sets you up for success because you are no longer in a state of slumber and sluggishness. Exercising first thing in the morning also has the added benefit of checking it off your list early so that you do not wait for the lazy bug to tell you not to enter the gym.

Sure getting up earlier to exercise might also be a struggle in of itself, but you do not necessarily have to travel to a gym far away to get your daily exercise. Simply stepping out of the house for a quick run or finding an empty space in your house where you will not be disturbed and begin a yoga routine that you can find on YouTube will also suffice. As long as you get the body moving and in a state of flow, you would have already won the day.

Putting exercise first above all else in your day also gives you a sense of accomplishment that you have taken the action to improve your health consistently. Losing excess body fat will also increase your energy levels and help you get through the challenges of your work day with greater ease.

If you find that exercising first thing in the morning is just impossible to do for some reason, make it a point to schedule it sometime before midday, preferably during your lunch break. Leaving exercise to the night will only trigger more excuses from your brain not to go as your will power gets depleted more and more throughout the day. From experience, unless I have booked a class that i can't back out of in the evening, more often than not I will find many more excuses not to go than if I had scheduled exercise early in the day.

If there is a sport that you particularly like, I also urge you to schedule more games with friends or family throughout the week as you are more likely to show up for them seeing that you already favour the sport over other exercises. In my case I love tennis and would almost never miss a session that I have scheduled. Gym and yoga on the other hand, I am more inclined to give it a miss if given the opportunity.

So for those of you who want to operate in a higher state of mind, body, and spirit, I challenge you to make exercise your number one priority and put it at the top of your list of things to do for the day. You will find your mind will be clearer and you will know exactly what you need to do for the day as you flow with the exercise. Feel free to play your favourite music playlist as you workout as well.

Chapter 34:

How To Find Motivation

Today we're going to talk about a topic that hopefully will help you find the strength and energy to do the work that you've told yourself you've wanted or needed to but always struggle to find the one thing that enables you to get started and keep going. We are going to help you find motivation.

In this video, I am going to break down the type of tasks that require motivation into 2 distinct categories. Health and fitness, and work. As I believe that these are the areas where most of you struggle to stay motivated. With regards to family, relationships, and other areas, i dont think motivation is a real problem there.

For all of you who are struggling to motivate yourself to do things you've been putting off, for example getting fit, going to the gym, motivation to stay on a diet, to keep working hard on that project, to study for your exams, to do the chores, or to keep working on your dreams... All these difficult things require a huge amount of energy from us day in and day out to be consistent and to do the work.

I know... it can be incredibly difficult. Having experienced these ups and downs in my own struggle with motivation, it always starts off swimmingly... When we set a new year's resolution, it is always easy to think that we will stick to our goal in the beginning. We are super motivated to go do the gym to lose those pounds, and we go every single day for about a week... only to give up shortly after because we either don't see results, or we just find it too difficult to keep up with the regime.

Same goes for starting a new diet... We commit to doing these things for about a week, but realize that we just simply don't like the process and we give up as well...

Finding motivation to study for an important exam or working hard on work projects are a different kind of animal. As these are things that have a deadline. A sense of urgency that if we do not achieve our desired result, we might fail or get fired from our company. With these types of tasks, most of us are driven by fear, and fear becomes our motivator... which is also not healthy for us as stress hormones builds within us as we operate that way, and we our health pays for it.

Let's start with tackling the first set of tasks that requires motivation. And i would classify this at the health and fitness level. Dieting, exercise, going to the gym, eating healthily, paying attention to your sleep... All these things are very important, but not necessarily urgent to many of us. The deadline we set for ourselves to achieve these health goals are arbitrary. Based on the images we see of models, or people who seem pretty fit around us, we set an unrealistic deadline for ourselves to achieve those body goals. But more often than not, body changes don't happen in days or weeks for most of us by the way we train. It could take up to months or years... For those celebrities and fitness models you see on Instagram or movies, they train almost all day by personal trainers. And their deadline is to look good by the start of shooting for the movie. For most of us who have day jobs, or don't train as hard, it is unrealistic to expect we can achieve that body in the same amount of time. If we only set aside 1 hour a day to exercise, while we may get gradually fitter, we shouldn't expect that amazing transformation to happen so quickly. It is why so many of us set ourselves up for failure.

To truly be motivated to keep to your health and fitness goals, we need to first define the reasons WHY we even want to achieve these results in the first place. Is it to prove to yourself that you have discipline? Is it to look good for your wedding photoshoot? Is it for long term health and fitness? Is it so that you don't end up like your relatives who passed too soon because of their poor health choices? Is it to make yourself more attractive so that you can find a man or woman in your life? Or is it just so that you can live a long and healthy life, free of medical complications that plague most seniors by the time they hit their 60s and 70s? What are YOUR reasons WHY you want to keep fit? Only after you know these reasons, will you be able to truly set a realistic deadline for your health goals. For those that are in it for a better health overall until their ripe old age, you will realize that this health goal is a life long thing. That you need to treat it as a journey that will take years and decades. And small changes each day will add up. Your motivator is not to go to the gym 10 hours a day for a week, but to eat healthily consistently and exercise regularly every single day so that you will still look and feel good 10, 20, 30, 50 years, down the road.

And for those that need an additional boost to motivate you to keep the course, I want you to find an accountability partner. A friend that will keep you in check. And hopefully a friend that also has the same health and fitness goals as you do. Having this person will help remind you not to let yourself and this person down. Their presence will hopefully motivate you to not let your guard down, and their honesty in pointing out that you've been slacking will keep you in check constantly that you will do as you say.

And if you still require an additional boost on top of that, I suggest you print and paste a photo of the body that you want to achieve and the idol that you wish to emulate in terms of having a good health and fitness on a board where you can see every single day. And write down your reasons why beside it. That way, you will be motivated everytime you walk past this board to keep to your goals always.

Now lets move on to study and work related tasks. For those with a fixed 9-5 job and deadlines for projects and school related work, your primary motivator right now is fear. Which as we established earlier, is not exactly healthy. What we want to do now is to change these into more positive motivators. Instead of thinking of the consequences of not doing the task, think of the rewards you would get if you completed it early. Think of the relief you will feel knowing that you had not put off the work until the last minute. And think of the benefits that you will gain... less stress, more time for play, more time with your family, less worry that you have to cram all the work at the last possible minute, and think of the good results you will get, the opportunities that you will have seized, not feeling guilty about procrastinations... and any other good stuff that you can think of. You could also reward yourself with a treat or two for completing the task early. For example buying your favourite food, dessert, or even gadgets. All these will be positive motivators that will help you get the ball moving quicker so that you can get to those rewards sooner. Because who likes to wait to have fun anyway?

Now I will move on to talk to those who maybe do not have a deadline set by a boss or teacher, but have decided to embark on a new journey by themselves. Whether it be starting a new business, getting your accounting done, starting a new part time venture.. For many of these tasks, the only motivator is yourself. There is no one breathing down your neck to get the job done fast and that could be a problem in itself. What should we do in that situation? I believe with this, it is similar to how we motivate ourselves in the heath and fitness goals. You see, sheer force doesn't always work sometimes. We need to establish the reasons why we want to get all these things done early in life. Would it be to fulfil a dream that we always had since we were a kid? Would it be to earn an extra side income to travel the world? Would it be to prove to yourself that you can have multiple streams of income? Would it to become an accomplished professional in a new field? Only you can define your reasons WHY you want to even begin and stay on this new path in the first place. So only you can determine why and how you can stay on the course to eventually achieve it in the end.

Similarly for those of you who need additional help, I would highly recommend you to get an accountability partner. Find someone who is in similar shoes as you are, whether you are an entrepreneur, or self-employed, or freelance, find someone who can keep you in check, who knows exactly what you are going through, and you can be each other's pillars of support when one of you finds yourself down and out. Or needs a little pick me up. There is a strong motivator there for you to keep you on course during the rough time.

And similar to health and fitness goal, find an image on the web that resonates with the goal you are trying to achieve. Whether it might be to buy a new house, or to become successful, i want that image to always be available to you to look at every single day. That you never forget WHY you began the journey. This constant reminder should light a fire in you each and everyday to get you out of your mental block and to motivate you to take action consistently every single day.

So I challenge each and every one of you to find motivation in your own unique way. Every one of you have a different story to tell, are on different paths, and no two motivators for a person are the same. Go find that one thing that would ignite a fire on your bottom everytime you look at it. Never forget the dream and keep staying the course until you reach the summit.

Lightning Source UK Ltd.
Milton Keynes UK
UKHW020631070222
398308UK00009B/393

9 789814 952828